Contents

Some words are shown in bold, **like this.**
You can find out what they mean by looking in the glossary.

Where is North America?

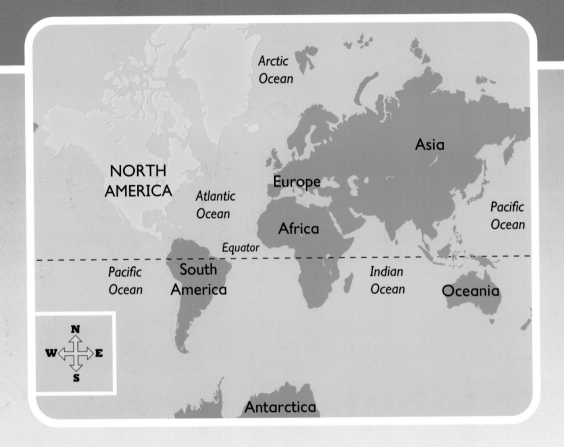

Arctic Ocean

Asia

NORTH AMERICA

Europe

Atlantic Ocean

Pacific Ocean

Africa

Equator

Pacific Ocean

South America

Indian Ocean

Oceania

N
W E
S

Antarctica

A continent is a vast mass of land that covers part of the Earth's surface. There are seven continents in the world, and North America is the third largest. In the north, North America stretches up beyond the **Arctic Circle**. In the south, it is joined to South America by a narrow strip of land.

North America

Mary Virginia Fox

www.heinemann.co.uk/library
Visit our website to find out more information about Heinemann Library books.

To order:

☎ Phone ++44 (0)1865 888066

🖹 Send a fax to ++44 (0)1865 314091

💻 Visit the Heinemann Bookshop at www.heinemann.co.uk/library to browse our catalogue and order online.

First published in Great Britain by Heinemann Library,
Halley Court, Jordan Hill, Oxford OX2 8EJ, a division of Reed
Educational and Professional Publishing Ltd. Heinemann is a
registered trademark of Reed Educational and Professional
Publishing Ltd.

OXFORD MELBOURNE AUCKLAND JOHANNESBURG
BLANTYRE GABORONE IBADAN PORTSMOUTH NH (USA)
CHICAGO

Designed by Depke Design
Originated by Dot Gradations
Printed by South China Printing in Hong Kong, China

06 05 04 03 02
10 9 8 7 6 5 4 3 2 1
ISBN 0 431 15792 8 (hardback)

07 06 05 04 03
10 9 8 7 6 5 4 3 2 1
SBN 0 431 15800 2 (paperback)

British Library Cataloguing in Publication Data
Fox, Mary Virginia
   North America. – (Continents)
   1.North America – Juvenile literature
   I.Title
   917

Acknowledgements
The publishers are grateful to the following for permission
to reproduce copyright material: Photo Edit/Myrleen
Ferguson, pp. 5, 26; Bruce Coleman, Inc./Dr. Eckart Pott, p. 7;
Earth Scenes/S. Osolinski, p. 9; Bruce Coleman, Inc./Bob Burch,
p. 11; Corbis/Scott T. Smith, p. 13; Bruce Coleman, Inc/M.P.L.
Fogden, p. 14; Bruce Coleman, Inc./Ed Degginger, p. 15; Bruce
Coleman, Inc./Peter French, p. 16; Bruce Coleman, Inc./Keith
Gunnar, p. 17; Bruce Coleman, Inc./J. Sarapochiello, p. 18;
Bruce Coleman, Inc./Sharon Smith, p. 20; Tony Stone/Joseph
Pobereskin, p. 21; Tony Stone/Donald Nausbaum, p. 22;
Earth Scenes/Eastcott/Momotiak/p. 24; Bruce Coleman, Inc./
J.C. Carton, p. 25; Photo Edit/Cindy Charles, p. 27; Tony
Stone/Doug Armand, p. 28.

Cover photo reproduced with permission of Science Photo
Library/Tom Van Sant, Geosphere Project/Planetary Visions.

Our thanks to Jane Bingham for her assistance in the
preparation of this book.

Every effort has been made to contact copyright holders
of any material reproduced in this book. Any omissions
will be rectified in subsequent printings if notice is given
to the Publisher.

Pacific coast, Oregon, USA

On either side of North America are two great oceans. To the west is the Pacific and to the east is the Atlantic. North America includes many islands. The large island of Greenland in the Arctic Ocean is part of the continent of North America, but it belongs to Denmark, in Europe.

Weather

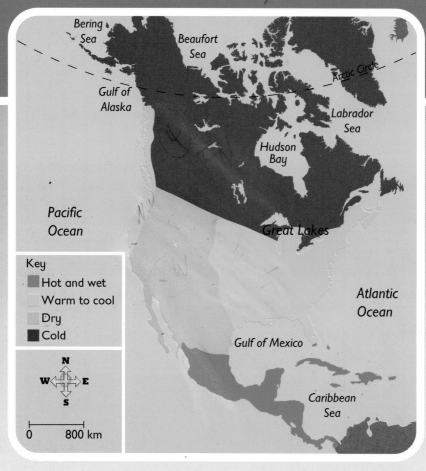

Bering Sea
Beaufort Sea
Gulf of Alaska
Arctic Circle
Labrador Sea
Hudson Bay
Pacific Ocean
Great Lakes
Atlantic Ocean

Key
Hot and wet
Warm to cool
Dry
Cold

N
W E
S

0   800 km

Gulf of Mexico
Caribbean Sea

North America has many different **climates**. In the south, the weather is very warm and it often rains. In the south west, there are deserts that bake in sunshine all year round. Further north, along the west coast of the United States, the weather is **mild**. Even in winter the sun shines most of the time.

Frozen ground in northern Canada

Near the **Arctic Circle**, in the far north, it is so cold that the ground stays frozen all year. Further south, around the Great Lakes, it is cold and snowy in winter, but the snow melts in summer. On the east coast of the United States, the weather is cold in winter but hot in summer.

Mountains and deserts

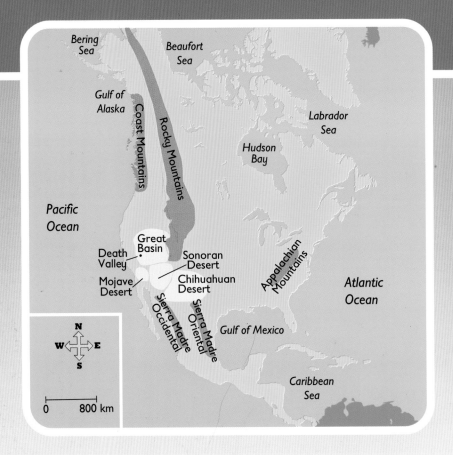

Bering Sea

Beaufort Sea

Gulf of Alaska

Coast Mountains

Rocky Mountains

Labrador Sea

Hudson Bay

Pacific Ocean

Great Basin

Death Valley

Mojave Desert

Sonoran Desert

Chihuahuan Desert

Sierra Madre Occidental

Sierra Madre Oriental

Appalachian Mountains

Atlantic Ocean

Gulf of Mexico

Caribbean Sea

N
W E
S

0   800 km

High mountain **ranges** run along the west of North America. The longest range stretches from the deserts of Mexico to the icy wastes of Alaska. For part of its length, this vast mountain range is known as the Rocky Mountains. The Appalachian Mountains in the east are much lower than the Rocky Mountains.

Sonoran Desert, New Mexico, USA

There are several large deserts in the southwestern United States and Mexico. These dry, stony places are baking hot in the daytime and bitterly cold at night. Death Valley in California is the hottest place in the USA. A temperature of 57°C has been recorded there.

Rivers

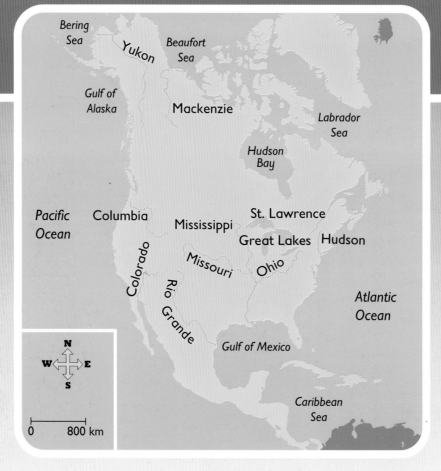

The Mississippi is one of the world's longest rivers. It starts near the Canadian border and flows south through the centre of the USA for 6020 kilometres. It empties into the Gulf of Mexico just beyond the city of New Orleans. Two other great rivers, the Missouri and the Ohio, run into the Mississippi.

Canal on the St Lawrence River

The St Lawrence River runs eastwards from the Great Lakes to the Atlantic Ocean. In some places, where the river runs downhill, **canals** have been built with **locks** to lift and lower boats safely from one level to another. This means that large ocean-going ships can travel along the river.

Lakes

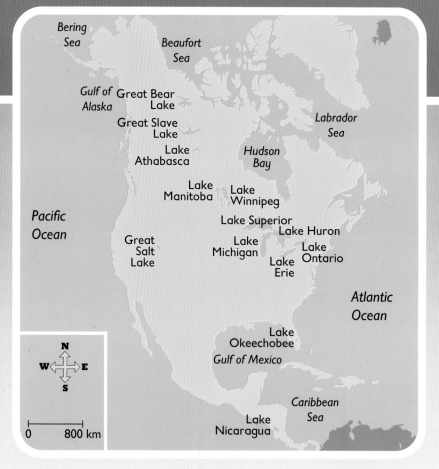

Bering
Sea

Beaufort
Sea

Gulf of Great Bear
Alaska Lake

Labrador
Sea

Great Slave
Lake

Lake
Athabasca

Hudson
Bay

Pacific
Ocean

Lake
Manitoba

Lake
Winnipeg

Lake Superior

Lake Huron

Great
Salt
Lake

Lake
Michigan

Lake
Ontario

Lake
Erie

Atlantic
Ocean

Lake
Okeechobee

Gulf of Mexico

N

W

E

S

Caribbean
Sea

0   800 km

Lake
Nicaragua

Five large **freshwater** lakes lie close to the **border** of the
USA and Canada. They are Lakes Superior, Michigan,
Huron, Erie and Ontario, and together they are known
as the Great Lakes. The lakes are linked to each other
by **canals**, and large ships can travel between them.

Great Salt Lake, Utah, USA

The Great Salt Lake is a shallow lake in a desert in western North America. Its water is so salty that swimmers can easily float in it. In very hot weather, the Great Salt Lake shrinks. Some of its water evaporates in the heat, and turns into water vapour in the air.

Animals

Bison in a national park, South Dakota, USA

Millions of bison, also known as buffalo, used to live on the grassy **plains** of North America. Now, most bison live in **national parks**, where they are protected from hunters. Golden eagles and pumas live in the mountains of the north. Alligators and turtles lurk in the swamps of Florida, in the south.

Polar bear in the Arctic

Beyond the **Arctic Circle,** in the far north of the continent, polar bears live on the ice. They hunt for fish in the water where there are breaks in the ice. Whales, walruses and seals swim in the icy Arctic Sea. In western Canada, grizzly bears live in caves in the mountains.

Plants

Redwood trees, California, USA

Giant redwood trees grow on the northwest coast of the United States. Redwoods are the tallest trees in the world – they can reach up to 112 metres tall. Maple trees grow in Canada and the northeast of the United States. People **tap** the trunks of maple trees to get sweet maple syrup.

Saguaro cactuses in the desert, Mexico

Many types of cactus grow in the deserts of the Southwest. Saguaro cactuses can be as tall as a four-storey building. Spiky Joshua trees are found in the higher and cooler parts of the deserts. They are incredibly tough and can live for up to 1000 years.

Languages

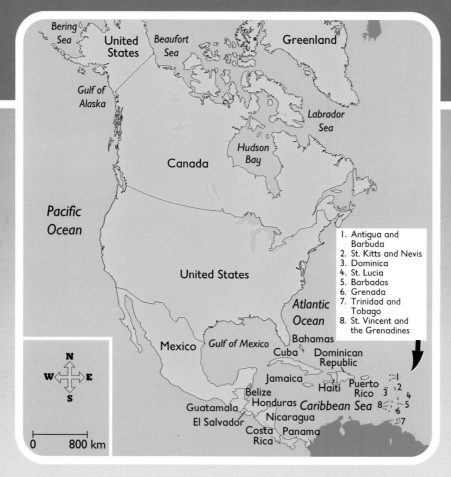

The first people living in North America were **Native Americans**. They had their own languages, but now only a few Native Americans speak these languages. Today, most people in the United States speak English. In some parts of Canada people speak French.

Shop in Oaxa City, Mexico

South of the United States is an area known as Central America. It contains seven countries. Central America stretches from below Mexico to the South American **border**. Most people in Central America speak Spanish. Spanish is spoken on some Caribbean islands too.

Cities

Mexico City, Mexico

Mexico City is the largest city in the continent of North America. It is an important **business** centre with many modern buildings. It also has lots of churches built by Spanish **settlers**. Underneath Mexico City are the ruins of a much older city, which belonged to an ancient people called the Aztecs.

Manhattan Island, New York

New York is one of the most important cities in the world. People from all over the world visit the city for business and fun. New York is famous for its tall skyscrapers. Many of these skyscrapers stand on an island called Manhattan. The **headquarters** of the **United Nations** is in New York.

Havana, Cuba

Havana is the **capital city** of Cuba, the biggest island in the Caribbean Sea. It was built by Spanish **settlers** about 500 years ago and has many old buildings. Havana is a lively centre for jazz musicians and singers. It has a large port and **exports** cigars, sugar, coffee and fruit.

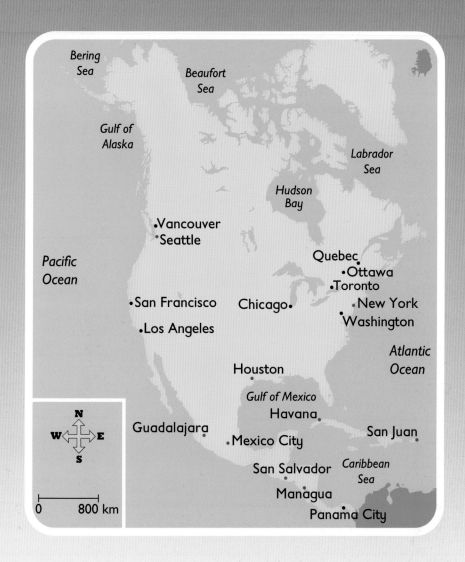

This map shows some of the main cities in the continent of North America. Toronto, in Canada, is a busy port on the shore of Lake Ontario. Large ships travel up the St Lawrence River to reach its harbour. Ottawa is the capital city of Canada; the Canadian **parliament** meets there.

 # In the country

Harvesting wheat in Alberta, Canada

North America has many kinds of countryside. In the centre of the continent are vast **plains** covered with wheat fields. Closer to the coasts, in the cooler grasslands, farmers raise herds of cattle. In the forests of Canada, people called lumberjacks cut down trees and saw them into logs.

Picking bananas in Costa Rica

On the northeast coast, people go fishing for cod and mackerel. Most fishing is done in large ships called **trawlers**. In the countries around the Caribbean Sea, the **climate** is good for growing coffee, sugar and bananas. These **crops** are grown on farms called **plantations**.

Famous places

Grand Canyon, Arizona, USA

The Grand Canyon is an incredibly steep and rocky river valley. It was formed over millions of years by the Colorado River. The river water cut through the rock to make the deep canyon sides. The Grand Canyon is 446 kilometres long and its walls have stripes of many colours.

Mayan pyramid, Tikal, Guatemala

The Maya people lived in Central America about 3500 years ago. They built stone cities deep in the forests. At the centre of these cities were temples shaped like pyramids, where the Maya worshipped their gods. The Maya studied the stars and invented their own system of writing, using pictures.

Niagara Falls, Ontario, Canada

The Niagara Falls form part of the **border** between the United States and Canada. They are actually two sets of waterfalls, the American Falls, in the USA, and the Horseshoe Falls, in Canada. Boats take visitors close to the crashing water.

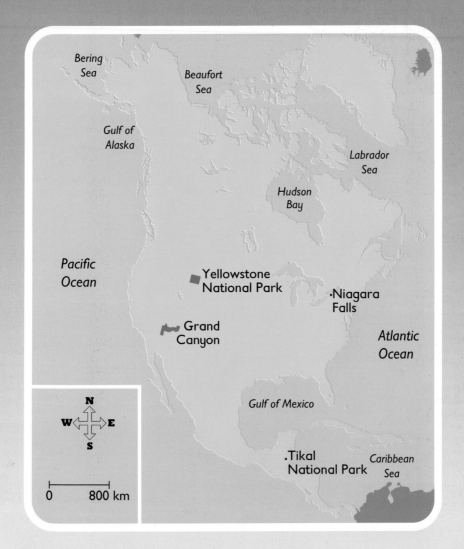

Bering Sea

Beaufort Sea

Gulf of Alaska

Labrador Sea

Hudson Bay

Pacific Ocean

Yellowstone National Park

·Niagara Falls

Grand Canyon

Atlantic Ocean

Gulf of Mexico

N
W←→E
S

0   800 km

·Tikal National Park

Caribbean Sea

Yellowstone Park, in the Rocky Mountains, is the oldest **national park** in the world. The Park contains hundreds of geysers – jets of hot steam that shoot up suddenly out of the ground. The most famous geyser in the park is Old Faithful. It sends out a spurt of steam about once every hour.

Fast facts

1. North America has the most kinds of climate of any continent.

2. The border between Canada and the USA is the world's longest land border between any two countries.

3. North America has the worlds shortest river! The Roe River, which flows into the River Missouri in the USA, is only 61 metres long.

4. Lake Superior on the border of Canada and the USA is the world's largest freshwater lake.

5. The Great Salt Lake in Utah is saltier than the oceans.

6. About 2000 different newspapers are published every day in North America.

7. The CN tower in Toronto is the tallest tower in the world. It is 553 metres tall.

8. The hottest temperature ever recorded in North America was 57°C in Death Valley, California in 1913.

Glossary

Arctic Circle imaginary line that circles the Earth near the North Pole

border dividing line between one country and another

business buying and selling of things

canal channel filled with water that ships go through

capital city city where government leaders work

climate kind of weather a place has

crops plants grown by farmers to be used as food

export to send goods to another country to be sold

freshwater water that is not salty

headquarters place from where something is run

lock closed-off part of a river or canal where boats are raised and lowered

mild warm but not hot

national park area of wild land protected by the government

Native Americans first people to live in North America

parliament group of people who make the laws of their country

plains large, flat areas of land

range line of connected mountains

settlers people who come to live in a country

tap to make a hole in a tree trunk and let out a liquid

trawler fishing boat that drags a bag-shaped net through the water

United Nations group of countries that works together for world peace

More books to read

An Illustrated Atlas of North America, Keith Lye, Cherrytree Books, 1999

Who Were the First North Americans?, Philippa Wingate, Usborne Publishing, 1995

North America, Cass Sandak, Hodder Wayland, 1997

Index